YOU CHOOSE

CAN YOU ESCAPE A HAUNTED HOUSE?

An Interactive Paranormal Adventure

by Ailynn Collins

CAPSTONE PRESS
a capstone imprint

Published by Capstone Press, an imprint of Capstone
1710 Roe Crest Drive, North Mankato, Minnesota 56003
capstonepub.com

Copyright © 2026 by Capstone. All rights reserved. No part of this publication
may be reproduced in whole or in part, or stored in a retrieval system, or
transmitted in any form or by any means, electronic, mechanical, photocopying,
recording, or otherwise, without written permission of the publisher.

Library of Congress Cataloging-in-Publication Data is available
on the Library of Congress website.
ISBN: 9798875210242 (hardcover)
ISBN: 9798875210211 (paperback)
ISBN: 9798875210228 (ebook PDF)

Summary: Readers explore haunted houses around the world and experience
paranormal activity that has been inspired by reports from real people.

Editorial Credits
Editor: Carrie Sheely; Designer: Elijah Blue; Media Researcher: Jo Miller;
Production Specialist: Tori Abraham

Photo Credits
Alamy: Graham Mulrooney, 45, ClassicStock, 33, Cotswolds Photo Library,
72, 74; Getty Images: David Wall, 62, 89, ilia-art, 94, iStock/scaliger, 100;
Shutterstock: Abramova Kseniya, 59 (horse legs), beerlogoff, 70, Debbie Ann
Powell, 40, Dragan Jovanovic, 13, James Kirkikis, 19, Lario Tus, 102, Maya
Kruchankova, 28, Photo Visions, cover (lightning), Raggedstone, 52, Roaming
Panda Photos, 106, Sabrina Janelle Gordon, cover (house), Teo Wei Keong,
76, Ulyana Vyugina, 46, Victoria Ditkovsky, 10, Volodya Senkiv, 6, Wirestock
Creators, 82

Design Elements
Capstone: Dina Her; Shutterstock: Nik Merkulov, Olha Nion,
Rifah Tasnia Tanisha

Any additional websites and resources referenced in this book are not
maintained, authorized, or sponsored by Capstone. All product and company
names are trademarks™ or registered® trademarks of their respective holders.

Printed and bound in China. 006276

TABLE OF CONTENTS

INTRODUCTION
About Your Adventure 5

CHAPTER 1
It's Not Goodbye Forever 7

CHAPTER 2
Winchester Mystery House 11

CHAPTER 3
Rose Hall Great House 41

CHAPTER 4
Ancient Ram Inn 73

CHAPTER 5
Haunted Houses 103

More Ghostly Encounters 106

Other Paths to Explore 108

Glossary 109

Select Bibliography 110

Read More 111

Internet Sites 111

About the Author 112

INTRODUCTION
ABOUT YOUR ADVENTURE

YOU are about to visit three different houses around the world. But don't expect them to be cozy and inviting. They all are known for being haunted! Face eerie experiences reported by people in each one. Can you escape a haunted house?

Chapter One sets the scene. Then you choose which path to read. Follow the directions at the bottom of the page. Your decisions will change your outcome. After you finish one path, go back and read the others for new perspectives and more adventures.

Turn the page to begin your adventure.

CHAPTER 1
IT'S NOT GOODBYE FOREVER

"I can't believe I'm losing both of you!" you cry.

Tyler and Maggie have been your best friends forever. Now they're both moving back to their hometowns. Tyler is headed to Jamaica, and Maggie is going back to England.

You talk about the summer camps you've all enjoyed and how the three of you would sit for hours around campfires listening to scary stories. When the other campers were too scared to keep listening, you three begged the counselors for more ghost stories.

Turn the page.

"Let's promise to visit each other real soon," you say. "We should look up the most haunted houses closest to us."

Maggie claps. "And we'll visit them together!"

"We'll get our fill of scares!" Tyler adds.

"It'll give us something to look forward to," you say as you hug them goodbye.

Later, you research some haunted houses. You are happy to find that there's one in your state only a few hours away. There's a whole community of people who love haunted houses.

There are even professional ghost hunters who use specialized equipment to find spirits. You share this information with your friends.

You take on small jobs and save up all your money. The following summer, your parents agree to take the family on vacation to Jamaica or England. If you want to see the haunted house nearest to you, Tyler and Maggie will return in the summer and stay with you. Where will you go first?

- To visit the Winchester Mystery House in California, turn to page 11.

- To visit Rose Hall in Jamaica, turn to page 41.

- To visit The Ancient Ram Inn in England, turn to page 73.

CHAPTER 2
WINCHESTER MYSTERY HOUSE

Your friends are spending the week with you back in the United States. After a fun car ride, you arrive at the Winchester Mystery House.

"This place doesn't look so scary," you remark when you arrive in the evening. Walking through the beautiful garden toward the front door, you pass between two statues near a fountain.

Turn the page.

The building looks like it's part house, part castle. There are many ornate decorations on the front. Some of the towers look like they're suspended in midair.

Inside, you meet Addie, the professional ghost hunter, along with three other adults.

"Welcome to the ghost tour," Addie begins. "I applaud you all for your bravery."

Maggie and Tyler gulp. Your heart beats faster.

Addie continues. "There are one hundred sixty rooms in this house. We won't get to all of them because we want to spend time in the more ghostly rooms. In these two hours, you may hear or see strange things."

She leads you down a long, narrow hallway and turns into another.

"There are many unusual things in this house, including doors that open to walls," she continues. "One opens to a twelve-foot drop."

You enter a large airy room. There are several pieces of stained glass on display and photos on the wall.

"This house was owned by Sarah Lockwood Pardee Winchester," Addie says. "In 1862, she married William Winchester. He made his fortune making and selling guns."

Turn the page.

A bedroom inside the Winchester Mystery House

She points to a photo of a woman on a horse-drawn cart. "This is a rare photo of Sarah Winchester," she says. "She rarely had photos taken."

"In 1866, William and Sarah had a baby girl," Addie says. "Tragically, the baby died five weeks later. In 1881, William, who had been ill for a long time, died."

She sighs before continuing. "Four years later, Sarah moved from their home in Connecticut to California. She bought a two-story farmhouse. This began a long remodeling process. By 1900, the farmhouse had become a seven-story Victorian mansion. The renovations to this house went on for thirty-six years. They stopped when Sarah died in 1922."

Your group walks up some low steps that go one way and then the other.

"These are called the switchback stairs because of the sharp turns," she explains. "There are forty-four steps with seven turns, and it runs one hundred feet. But all that only leads to the second floor, nine feet above the last floor. Sarah had crippling arthritis, so low steps made it easier for her to get from one floor to the next."

Addie turns around. "The year after Sarah's death, the house was opened to visitors. There were many stories of ghostly encounters. According to the stories, Sarah's medium claimed that the ghosts were people killed by the guns that William made."

She pauses at a table with equipment on it. "These are supplies that ghost hunters use. Please pick one."

Turn the page.

Addie shows you the night-vision camera. There's also a machine to record sounds and an EMF detector. It picks up changes in the electromagnetic field.

Tyler picks up an infrared thermometer. "If there's a ghost in the room, the temperature will drop, right? I read that somewhere."

Addie nods.

You decide on the binary-response device. Addie says this is a way for you to ask ghosts a question. They answer with a yes or no.

Maggie chooses the radio-frequency scanner. "If it beeps, a ghost might be nearby," Addie tells her. "The more it beeps, the closer you are to it."

"Now that we're equipped, we'll be visiting three main rooms—the basement, Sarah's bedroom, and the Grand Ballroom," Addie says. "These rooms have had many paranormal reports. It's best if we all stick together, okay?"

She leads the group through twists and turns of hallways. You lose track of where you are.

As you fall behind the group, a shadow crosses your side. You turn to look, but nothing's there. After a few more steps, you see it again! This time, the shadow flits over you on the ceiling.

Your curiosity is piqued. This could be a chance to ask a ghost a question with your device. But Addie said to stick together.

- To sneak away, turn to page 18.
- To stay with the group, turn to page 25.

Your curiosity is so strong that you have to follow the shadow. You want Maggie and Tyler to go with you, but they've already moved on.

The shadow leads you through more hallways and doors. It glides upstairs to the third floor. You stop in a room with a triangular roof like an attic. It has two small windows at each end.

The shadow stops by the farthest window in the room. It seems to take on the form of a woman. She's dressed in old-fashioned black clothing. She looks longingly out the window. You can't believe your eyes. Is this an actual ghost? Could it be Sarah herself?

Suddenly, something lands on your shoulder. You scream and turn around to find Addie staring at you. She looks annoyed.

"I found Sarah!" you blurt out.

"You did? Where?" Addie asks.

You turn back to point to the shadow at the window, but she's gone.

Addie gives you a look that says she doesn't believe you. You think about telling her more, but out of the corner of your eye, you see the shadow again. Addie motions for you to follow her. But Sarah's ghost is heading the other way.

Stairs leading to an upper floor of the Winchester Mystery House

- To follow the shadow again, turn to page 20.
- To go with Addie, turn to page 22.

You wait until Addie is several feet ahead and turn down a different hallway. Sarah's ghost headed toward a back room. You move as quietly as you can through a dining room and through another door.

The room you step into is dark. There are light curtains covering the windows. There's just enough moonlight coming through so you can see. Sarah sits by a cradle, singing to it as if rocking a baby to sleep.

You're filled with a heaviness as if all the energy has been sucked out of your body. You want to cry.

"You lost your baby," you whisper. It isn't really a question, but the green light glows on your device. You're making a connection with this ghost!

She turns to face you. Her face is hideous as if all the life has drained from it. She raises a hand toward you. Her thin skeletal fingers grasp at the air. She is trying to grab you! You stumble backward and out of the room. You run right into Addie again. She's really angry this time.

"I can't keep you safe if we don't stick together," she huffs. "We're about to see Sarah's bedroom."

"I'm sorry," you cry. "Let's get out of here."

"The tour isn't over yet," Addie says, pulling you back toward the stairs. "If you stick with the group, you'll be fine."

Tyler and Maggie might be mad if you abandon them before the tour ends. But part of you feels like you've had enough of this.

• To see Sarah's bedroom, turn to page 22.
• To leave the tour, turn to page 36.

Addie leads you down the hallway into Sarah's bedroom. There's a large bed and some chairs. The windows are framed by heavy, burgundy curtains.

Maggie glances at you. "You disappeared," she whispers. "You need to stick with us, okay? This is getting scary."

"Look at this old piano," Tyler says as he runs his fingers over the keys. He plays some notes, filling the room with an eerie sound.

Addie gathers the tour group around her. "There have been signs of supernatural activity here in the past. Let's be very quiet."

You look at the piano. Two men hover quietly over the fireplace next to the instrument. They look like they're doing repairs on the fireplace. When did they get here?

You tug on Tyler's arm and point, feeling annoyed that workers would be here to interfere with the ghost hunt.

"What?" Tyler says. When he looks, the men are gone.

You couldn't have imagined them. They were so real!

"What's the matter?" Maggie whispers. Before you can answer, the scanner in her hands begins to beep. Maggie jumps. She throws the scanner to you.

Holding the scanner, you move over to the fireplace. The closer you get, the more the scanner beeps.

Addie's eyes grow wide. "It's never beeped that much before!"

Turn the page.

She faces the fireplace. "Spirit, we are here to visit and mean no harm. Are you okay with our presence?"

You look down at your device. Nothing happens. You let out a sigh of relief.

"Maybe they've left," Addie says, disappointed. She waits a while for another response. When no one gets a reading on their devices, she shrugs. "Let's head to the ballroom then. We should get better readings there."

You're spooked after seeing the workers' ghosts. You want to leave. But Maggie and Tyler haven't seen anything unusual yet. You don't want to disappoint them. Maybe you should stay.

- To go to the Grand Ballroom, turn to page 27.
- To leave and head outside alone, turn to page 30.

The stairs are steep and dark. You are all silent. You focus on not tripping or running into the person in front of you.

The basement is a labyrinth of brick-walled hallways. You cling to your friends. You don't want to get lost down here.

"This is one of two basements," Addie says. She points to the right. "Down those steps, you can see the boiler. She turns to the left. "And that's called steam alley because that's where the radiators are found. A worker is said to still wander around here. We call him the wheelbarrow ghost."

Someone taps you on the shoulder.

"What is it?" you ask. But no one's there.

"My scanner is beeping," Maggie whispers.

Turn the page.

"And my thermometer shows it's getting colder in here," Tyler says.

Addie heads to the boiler. She takes the few steps down into that area.

"Is the wheelbarrow ghost here?" you ask.

The green light on your device lights up. Yes! There is a ghost here.

"Come on," Maggie says as she motions for you to follow Addie. But your feet are frozen. The wheelbarrow ghost is in here, and he's answering your questions.

- To see the boiler, turn to page 33.
- To keep talking to the ghost, turn to page 37.

You follow the others out and pass several unfinished rooms.

Addie continues telling you about the house. "There are more than ten thousand windows, two thousand doors, forty-seven fireplaces, forty-seven staircases, thirteen bathrooms, and six kitchens," she says.

Everyone gasps at these numbers.

You arrive at the ballroom. "This is my favorite room," Addie says. "There are some fun features here."

The Grand Ballroom is lavishly decorated. There's a large fireplace at one end, elaborate red wallpaper, and beautiful wooden wall panels. Addie gathers the group in the middle of the room. She signals for silence, and you all wait for something to happen.

Turn the page.

Tyler shivers. He looks down at the device in his hand. "The temperature is dropping," he says.

Addie grins. "Spirits, are you here?"

You check your device. A green light blinks. Other devices react. Maggie's is beeping quietly. Addie turns on her camera, hoping to capture video of something.

The lit candles in the room all go out, as if a cold breath has blown them out at once.

"I have a flashlight," Addie says reassuringly. She switches it on.

A beam of light brings you some comfort until it lights up the face of a man. It's more like half a face. The other half looks like it's been blown off. And he's standing right behind Addie! Everyone in the tour group screams and scrambles to get out.

As soon as you are clear of the house and standing in the gardens, you let out the breath you were holding. Others in the group are pale with fear.

The three of you meet your parents in the parking lot. When they ask about the night, you tell them, "So much happened. I promise to tell you all about it when we get home." You can't wait to get away from here.

THE END

To follow another path, turn to page 9.
To learn more about haunted houses, turn to page 103.

"If you're not feeling well, go ahead and wait for us outside," Maggie says. You can tell she'd rather you stay, but she's being a good friend.

You step out into the night air and take in a deep breath. The smell of the garden makes you feel better. You spot a bench in a corner.

A young boy dressed in old-fashioned clothing sits on one end of the bench. You wonder if he's in costume for the tourists.

"Hi," you say, trying to be polite. "Mind if I sit here with you?"

The boy shrugs.

You pull out your cell phone and text your parents. The boy seems interested in what you're doing.

"Just texting my parents," you say. "They're coming to get me soon."

The boy's eyebrows furrow, as if he doesn't understand you. You show him your phone screen, not wanting to be impolite.

The boy jumps away from your phone. "What evil is this?"

"My phone?" you ask, puzzled.

The boy rises up off the bench, his feet actually leaving the ground. That's when you realize you can see right through him. He's floating above you.

You don't stop to wonder what's going on. You run for the front entrance, tripping over a few tree roots.

Turn the page.

When you reach the street, your parents' car pulls up.

"Where are your friends?" Mom asks.

You tell them you left the tour early. "It was more than I bargained for. The rest will be out soon."

When Maggie and Tyler emerge from the tour, they aren't annoyed as you expected them to be. In fact, they look pale and shaken by the experience. Nobody says a word all the way back to the hotel. It will be days before the three of you can talk about what happened at the Winchester Mystery House.

THE END

To follow another path, turn to page 9.
To learn more about haunted houses, turn to page 103.

You stick with your friends. There's strength in numbers, you tell yourself.

Everyone stops in front of the boiler. It's large and black with an opening at the bottom. This is where the coal was fed into the boiler. After several minutes, Addie opens a wooden door nearby. You expect to see a room, but instead, there's nothing but a brick wall.

Many homes used coal-burning furnaces in the early 1900s.

"Sarah liked to put these blocked doors everywhere in the house," Addie explains. "I think she wanted to confuse the spirits."

"And the people," Tyler adds, trying to laugh.

You all stand still again with your shoulders touching. You hold out your instruments, hoping something will happen as it did before.

Nothing.

It suddenly feels like you've been standing there for half an hour. Addie asks the spirits questions, but the device in your hands remains silent.

"Sarah, are you here?" Addie tries again. "What about victims of Will's guns?"

Maggie sighs loudly and that seems to annoy Addie.

"The spirits aren't always at our beck and call," she snaps. "It also depends on how receptive we all are. Maybe no one really wants to meet a spirit tonight."

Shaking her head, Addie leads you all back up to the main level. Because you spent so long in the basement, there isn't much time to linger in the rest of the house.

You admire the house as you walk through. As everyone exits, you see your parents waiting for you. You, Maggie, and Tyler chat happily about the tour all the way back to the hotel. You are secretly glad that nothing really happened tonight.

THE END

To follow another path, turn to page 9.
To learn more about haunted houses, turn to page 103.

35

You thought you were brave, but really, you're not. Meeting one ghost—the main ghost—was enough.

"I'm going to wait for you all at the front door," you say.

No matter what Addie says, you won't change your mind. She leaves you in a huff.

You sit on a bench in the beautiful garden. You admire the house from the outside, relieved. When your friends emerge at the end of the night, you listen quietly to their stories. You can't wait to tell them of how you met Sarah's ghost. But you might wait until tomorrow. You're still having a hard time believing it yourself.

THE END

To follow another path, turn to page 9.
To learn more about haunted houses, turn to page 103.

"I'll catch up in a minute," you tell Maggie.

"Are you one of the people who lived in this house?" you ask the ghost.

The red light goes on.

"Were you killed by one of the Winchester guns?"

The green light goes on and off.

Sarah's medium was right. The victims of the guns are haunting the house.

A hand touches you on your shoulder. You jump. It's Tyler.

"The temperature on this side of the basement is colder than over there," he says in a low voice. "Do you feel chilly?"

You tell him what you've been doing. His eyes light up. "Ask if they're dangerous," he suggests.

Turn the page.

You ask, and both lights go on. What does that mean?

"Maybe we should get out of here," Tyler says.

You have a million questions to ask the ghost, but your mind is blank now.

Addie calls across the room. "You two please stick with the group." She sounds impatient.

"But—," you stammer. You try to tell her you've got a ghost here, but she doesn't seem to want to hear you.

A good question pops into your head. "Do you—," you begin.

A rush of freezing wind crosses over you. You lose your balance and fall back against the hard wall. You hit your head. The room spins, and you slide down onto the floor.

Addie and everyone in the group surrounds you in alarm. Voices echo all around. You can't focus.

Finally, someone picks you up in their arms. As you leave the basement, you're sure you spot someone standing by the boiler. They're wearing old-fashioned clothing that's splattered in blood.

You want to scream, but your head hurts too much. You shut your eyes. The next thing you know, you're in your parents' car on the way to the hospital. You'll never forget your visit to the Winchester Mystery House.

THE END

To follow another path, turn to page 9.
To learn more about haunted houses, turn to page 103.

CHAPTER 3
ROSE HALL GREAT HOUSE

"Are you ready to be scared out of your skin?" Tyler asks.

You and your parents have been enjoying the beaches of Montego Bay, Jamaica. Today, you, Tyler, and Maggie will visit Rose Hall, the most haunted house on this island.

The tour bus picks you up at your hotel after dinner. You and your friends chatter excitedly all the way there. When you reach the main entrance, your jaw drops.

Turn the page.

The long, winding road to the house goes through a beautifully landscaped golf course. Majestic trees line both sides of the road as you approach.

"Rose Hall sits on six thousand six hundred acres," Tyler tells you. "The land around it used to be a sugar plantation."

When the bus stops, you step out onto a stone walkway. The large house is three stories high with many windows. A large balcony juts out from the front. An arched door behind it is open and dark. The setting sun lights up the house in a warm, yellow glow.

You look up and see something white flicker past the dark doorway. Are there actors playing the roles of ghosts?

At the top of the stairs, you meet Yvonne, your guide for the night. She wears a long, flowing dress with a wide white collar and greets you with a grin.

"Welcome," she says to the group that's gathered. There are about 15 people, including you and your friends. "You've chosen to come to the night visit. I hope you have the courage to complete this tour. If not, please know that you can always come back here and wait." She points to several stone benches along the edge of the landing.

"Do you think we'll make it to the end?" Maggie asks nervously.

You nod confidently. "We don't scare so easily."

Turn the page.

Yvonne opens her arms wide. "The great house you see before you is a perfect restoration of the original Rose Hall. But I'm sure you want to know the legends about Annee Palmer, the mysterious woman who lived in this great house."

"Yes," you reply quietly.

"The Englishman John Palmer came to our island to seek his fortune," Yvonne continues. "He bought this plantation. He later married Annee, who came to be known as the White Witch of Rose Hall. The stories say Annee was raised in Haiti by a nanny who knew a lot about voodoo. People believed Annee practiced dark magic as well. The legend says that Annee eventually killed three husbands and several enslaved people who lived on her plantation."

"How did she get away with that?" you ask, stunned by the story.

Bedroom in Rose Hall Great House

"Well, she may not have," Yvonne says, shaking her head. "According to some stories, Annee was murdered by the enslaved people. In addition, to prevent her ghost from rising from the dead, they burned down her house. They buried her in a large tomb and marked crosses on its sides to keep her spirit inside."

Yvonne sighs. "Unfortunately, those that buried her didn't complete the ritual. Because of that, it's said her ghost still haunts the house and grounds. Even the restoration of the house didn't keep the ghost away."

Turn the page.

"So, would you prefer to begin the tour inside the house or in the gardens?" Yvonne asks. "The room we start with is what we like to call one of the safest rooms in the house. Very few incidents have occurred there. The tomb is in the garden, though, and that is a rather spiritual place."

Yvonne tells the group that if they'd like to see the tomb first, they can follow the path to the back garden. Yvonne hands out lanterns to those who choose to go there.

You and Tyler can't wait for the fright of walking the dark path. But Maggie wants to start in the safe room. They agree to go where you choose.

- To enter the safe room, go to page 47.
- To visit the tomb, turn to page 51.

Yvonne leads you into a grand hall with many pieces of furniture on display. Chandeliers hang from the ceiling, and there are candlesticks on mantels and tables. Doorways from this hall lead to other darkened rooms. Yvonne lights the candlesticks that flicker in the stillness of the night.

Eerie.

"This main hall has been restored to look as it did when Annee Palmer lived here," Yvonne explains. "It's the safest room because very few sightings have occurred here. If we're quiet, we'll hear the house settling down for the night."

Sure enough, you hear creaks and pops.

"How do we know it's the house and not the spirits?" Maggie whispers nervously.

Yvonne overhears. "That's a good question."

Turn the page.

"Look!" Tyler points to something down one dark hallway. Everyone turns to see a woman in a white nightgown disappear through it. She has long hair that flows behind her.

"Who was that?" you ask.

Yvonne shrugs. "Who was what?" But her expression tells you she knows exactly what you're talking about.

As you step into the dining room, it feels like someone is watching you. You dismiss it as your imagination.

A chandelier above clinks as the glass teardrops knock into each other. There's no breeze coming through the room, so what made the chandelier move? You grab Maggie's hand.

Maggie gasps. "You're squeezing too hard. It hurts."

"Sorry!" you say as you let go.

"This is the library," Yvonne says, walking into the third room. "Back then, the men would sit here after dinner to talk. In the daytime, Annee would spend time in here reading."

You walk over to a painting of a pretty woman on the far wall.

"That's Annee Palmer," Yvonne says.

You linger at the painting. It's creepy how her eyes seem to follow you as you move to the left and right.

You turn to leave the room with the others and find that you're alone. The temperature plunges, and it's as cold as ice.

A low voice moans, but you can't make out the words.

Turn the page.

"What are you saying?" you ask.

The room fills up with smoke, but it has no smell. Your vision is blurred by the rising mist. Suddenly, someone is shaking you.

"Are you okay?" It's Maggie. She's looking at you with worry. "I told you to stick with me."

"Sorry," you say, shaking your head. Everything comes back into focus. Yvonne and the group have moved on.

"They've gone upstairs to her bedroom," Maggie says. "But I think you need a break. Let's go outside for some air."

Maggie may be right. You can't stop shivering. But you also want to see Annee's bedroom.

- To go outside for some air, turn to page 58.
- To continue to Annee's bedroom, turn to page 65.

Even though you'd love to see the inside of the house, the idea of the tomb is intriguing. You, Tyler, and Maggie join three other adults and head to Annee's tomb.

Using your battery-powered lamps, you walk through the gardens. You follow a stone path and head toward a clearing surrounded by tall trees. In the middle of the clearing is a concrete tomb. It's smaller than you expected. There are white crosses painted on three sides.

"They didn't paint a cross on the fourth side," Tyler says. "That's why they say her spirit was able to escape and haunt the grounds."

Someone touches your shoulder. You turn, expecting it to be Maggie, but no one is there.

When you turn back to tell Tyler, he's gone too. You're alone. Did your friends wander off?

Turn the page.

You don't like being alone, but you're afraid to leave the area in case they come back looking for you here.

- To stay at the tomb, go to page 53.
- To go looking for Tyler and Maggie, turn to page 68.

"Tyler! Maggie!" you call. You're sure they'll show up soon. They wouldn't leave you here alone, would they?

You walk around the tomb touching the white crosses. Someone shrieks in anger. The sound comes from behind you. You whip around.

You see the ghost of a woman floating above the tomb.

"Why have you disturbed me?" the woman demands.

Okay, this is too much. To make things worse, the ghost flies at you. You step aside quickly and put your foot down at a bad angle. Your ankle twists, and you fall down. You catch yourself with your hands, but land on rough stone.

Turn the page.

"Ouch!" you squeal.

The ghost shrieks angrily.

You scramble to your feet and try to run away. But your ankle is badly twisted. Pain shoots through you with every step.

"Help!" you cry.

"Go!" the ghost screeches. She flies at you again.

Your heart is pounding so fast now you can hardly breathe. You need to get away. But what if she chases you? Flying is obviously faster than running, especially with a hurt ankle.

- To run away, go to page 55.
- To face the ghost, turn to page 61.

Heading for the house, you run as fast as your twisted ankle allows you to.

Whoosh! The ghost flies at you.

Thud! Your foot catches on something hard and you trip, falling on your face. A wicked cackle echoes in the air. You get up on your hands and knees and crawl as fast as you can. You don't know which way you're headed, but you don't care.

Clambering up onto your feet, you spot an old shed ahead. The door is open. Inside, it's empty. You shut the door and crouch under the only window. You try to catch your breath.

The sound of hooves fills your ears. Someone is riding a horse outside. Peeking out the small window, you see a woman in a black cloak on a horse. You freeze.

Turn the page.

The thunder of hooves stops very suddenly. It's followed by the angry snort of a horse. The door to the shed flies open. A dark shadow stands at the doorway. The ghost has come for you.

You take a deep breath and prepare to scream at the top of your lungs.

"What are you doing in here?" It's Tyler's voice. "I've been looking everywhere for you."

You almost collapse in relief.

"I'm so glad it's you," you say, standing up gingerly.

"Who else would it be?" he says. "Everyone is waiting for us at the bus."

"Have I been gone that long?" The tour has only just started.

"It's been two hours since we were at the tomb," he says, scratching his head. "You're great at hiding."

You shake your head all the way back to the bus. You didn't hide on purpose, and somehow time has moved on faster than you can account for.

On the bus, Maggie has a thousand questions.

"I promise to tell you all about it," you say. You look back at the great house as it gets smaller with each passing second. "As soon as I figure out what happened."

THE END

To follow another path, turn to page 9.
To learn more about haunted houses, turn to page 103.

Tyler follows you and Maggie outside. "This is spookier than I expected," he says.

It's dark and cold outside.

"Let's wait here for the others," you suggest, walking to a stone bench. The three of you look up at the great house.

"Do you think Annee's spirit really haunts this place still?" Maggie asks. "It's been a long time, and this isn't even the original house. Surely, she's moved on."

For a second time tonight, something white flits across the open balcony doorway. You shiver. Is that Annee's ghost?

You stand. In the distance, you see smoke or a mist rising into the air.

"What is that?" you say, pointing.

"I'm not sure," Maggie replies. "Let's go check it out."

The path is dark. You pull out your cell phones to use the flashlight apps.

Then you hear the pounding of feet like a horse galloping. Or is it your heart?

"Let's get out of here!" you yell. You and your friends run back to the main house. You bump right into Yvonne, who glares at you in anger.

Turn the page.

"You should stick with the group," she says.

You tell her about the mist you saw and the sound of pounding hooves.

Yvonne's eyes go wide. "That might have been Annee riding around. Supposedly, her ghost rides a horse around the property," she says.

You look at your friends. All three of you are now officially freaked out.

Ignoring Yvonne's suggestion to rejoin the group, you run to the bus and climb aboard. You and your friends refuse to get out again until you're back at your hotel.

It's a long time before any of you can talk about what happened at Rose Hall.

THE END

To follow another path, turn to page 9.
To learn more about haunted houses, turn to page 103.

You came to encounter ghosts. It could be a trick, or it could be real. But this is an opportunity you cannot pass up.

With these thoughts, you realize all your fear has disappeared. You stare at the floating woman. She glares back, mumbling strange words.

"You can't put a curse on me," you declare. "I don't believe in those, and you've been dead for a long time."

The woman throws her head back and cackles. She continues to chant. The sound echoes through the trees. Chills run through you, but you refuse to be afraid.

"Fine," you snap. "Then I curse you back!"

Turn the page.

The ghost rises higher, spreading her arms as if to intimidate you. But you won't back down. You think of the worst possible curse that can be put on a ghost.

"I curse you to be here for all eternity, even when no one is here to be scared by you," you begin.

The woman jerks back several feet, as if she's been yanked by some invisible force.

"No!" she cries.

There's something pitiful in her expression. As you both stare at each other, you begin to feel sorry for her. What a terrible fate you've just placed on her. What if it means the ghost can never move on from its earthly existence?

"I'm sorry," you say. "Can I take it back?"

The ghost's face softens for just a moment. She doesn't look so scary. Suddenly, she rises up into the night sky and disappears.

You hear footsteps.

"Hey, why are you still here?" Tyler walks up behind you. "Everyone else has gone to see the house. Aren't you coming?"

Turn the page.

Your heart is still racing from your encounter with Annee Palmer.

"The house? Yes, of course," you say. "I'm coming."

You follow your friends to meet up with Yvonne.

"Ready to see the inside of Rose Hall?" she asks.

You nod. After that encounter, you don't think there's going to be anything in the house that could scare you now.

THE END

To follow another path, turn to page 9.
To learn more about haunted houses, turn to page 103.

You follow the group up the beautifully carved staircase into Annee's bedroom.

"Annee really loved red," Yvonne says, pointing to the red walls.

As soon as you step inside, the sound of a man moaning in pain fills your ears.

"Are you piping sound effects into the room?" you ask Yvonne.

"Not at all," she says. "Do you hear something unusual?"

You don't have time to answer because something white flashes past the bedroom door. You see a woman hurrying down the stairs.

"Do you have actors playing ghosts?" you ask.

Yvonne's eyes widen. "Absolutely not! Why would we do that?"

Turn the page.

Tyler swallows. "I think we should leave this room."

"Agreed," you say.

You both take a step back away from the bed.

"Where did everyone go?" you say. You and Tyler are alone in the room, and the door has been shut. A man appears, lying still on the bed.

You turn the doorknob to get out, but it won't budge. "It's locked," you say.

Tyler tries. He can't turn the knob, so he bangs on the door. "Let us out!" he calls.

Suddenly, the man on the bed sits up. Like a robot, his head turns slowly toward you. His empty eyes are terrifying. You help Tyler in banging on the door.

The door swings open. A security guard stands there, hands on hips, glaring.

"There you both are!" he says. "Yvonne is looking for you."

When you're reunited with the others, Maggie says that you and Tyler disappeared from the group, but they didn't notice until after the tour was over. "You were gone for hours," she says.

You can't explain any of that. You're quite sure you didn't deliberately leave the group. You may never know the truth about what happened, but you're sure you've had enough of ghosts.

THE END

To follow another path, turn to page 9.
To learn more about haunted houses, turn to page 103.

Where have your friends gone? You spot Tyler behind a large tree as if he's hiding from someone.

"What's going on?" you say, approaching.

Tyler turns to you with a finger on his lips. His eyes are wide with fear.

You follow his gaze. On the other side of the tree are three thin men. They're barefoot and carrying sticks and lit torches. They look terrified and determined.

"Those are enslaved people," Tyler whispers.

That's when the ground thunders under your feet. *Gallump! Gallump!*

Behind you, a dark horse gallops toward the men at full speed. It's being ridden by a woman wearing a long, flowing cloak. She shrieks and curses at the men.

The men don't run, even though you're sure she could do them some real harm. Instead, they rise up to meet her with their torches.

The horse rears up on its hind legs. The woman is thrown from the saddle, and she falls onto the hard ground. The men surround her, and you can't bear to watch. All you hear are screams and shouts of anger.

"Let's get out of here," Tyler says, terrified.

You both run for the house as fast as you can. As you take the stairs two at a time, you're greeted by the rest of your tour group. Yvonne is giving people directions to the tomb.

Panting, you try to explain that there's something terrible happening nearby.

"Are actors reenacting the murder of Annee Palmer?" you ask Yvonne.

Turn the page.

Yvonne ushers the group toward the path. "I assure you that nothing of the sort has been arranged for tonight," she replies. "You must have a very sensitive spirit," she whispers to you. "Not many have seen what you just described. People who reported seeing it have been terrified."

On the bus back to the hotel, you ask Tyler if he thinks you both imagined that scene. Your friend looks at you, bewildered.

"I didn't see anything unusual," he says. "I don't know what you're talking about."

That sends more chills up your spine. How could Tyler not remember what you both saw?

You're just glad to be getting out of here. You've had enough ghostly encounters for a long time.

THE END

To follow another path, turn to page 9.
To learn more about haunted houses, turn to page 103.

CHAPTER 4
ANCIENT RAM INN

It's summer, and your family is on vacation in England. This is your chance to visit Maggie. Tyler is going to be there too.

Maggie lives in a village called Wotton-under-Edge. It's a lovely, old village with stone cottages and narrow streets.

What's better is that one of the most haunted houses in the country is right up the street from Maggie's home. The three of you will get to spend one night at this house with a guide.

Turn the page.

The Ancient Ram Inn, Maggie's parents tell you, was built around 1145. It had several different uses before becoming an inn and pub.

You arrive at the inn just before 9:00 p.m. when the tour begins. The L-shaped inn looks its age. It's smaller than you pictured.

Ancient Ram Inn

"This could be quite cozy," you say. You glance up at the steeply slanted roof and chimneys jutting up into the night air.

You expected to see a large group of ghost hunters. But you three are the only ones here tonight. The guide is a young man named Sam.

"It looks like you three will get the VIP treatment tonight—from me and possibly from the spirits," Sam says after he introduces himself.

You put your overnight bags by the front door. Sam begins with some history of the place. He points to the wall behind you. It's filled with newspaper clippings of stories of hauntings experienced by people at the inn.

"This whole area used to be wetlands," he says. "And legend has it that it was used as an ancient burial ground. Have you heard of Stonehenge?"

Turn the page.

Historians believe Stonehenge was built in stages starting about 5,000 years ago.

You all nod. "We visited it just last week," you say. You loved Stonehenge. It felt so mysterious.

Sam smiles. "It is believed that two ley lines, stemming directly from Stonehenge, cross right here under this building."

"What's a ley line?" Tyler asks.

"Ley lines contain very high amounts of spiritual energy," Sam says. "The cross section of these lines is said to create a portal to the paranormal. People believe that's why spirits in this house are so strong, and maybe even dangerous."

"Dangerous?" Maggie says. "I didn't know that bit."

"It's believed that the house is built over a five-thousand-year-old burial site," Sam says. "When it was first built, it housed workers who were building St. Mary's Church across the street. A river had to be redirected. When natural waterways have to be moved, it's said the land gets more dark energy. So, there's a lot of potential for paranormal activity." His eyes glow in the dim lamplight.

He continues. "This house was bought in the 1960s by a man named John Humphries. He died in 2017, leaving it to his daughter, Caroline. According to John, the spirits here can be violent. He was dragged out of bed and thrown across the room. And that's just one story."

You gulp. Your friends look nervous too.

Turn the page.

Sam chuckles. "Don't worry. If you need anything, don't hesitate to come find me."

With that, Sam leads you up to your bedroom. It's a long, narrow room. The bedspreads are red, as are the curtains. You place your bags on the beds.

"Feel free to head to the kitchen area for some snacks," Sam says. "I have to close up the inn for the night. I'll meet you in the lobby in an hour." He walks out, leaving you three alone.

Tyler declares that he's a little hungry. Maggie would like to wash up first. You insist that the three of you stick together. Tyler and Maggie let you have the deciding vote on what to do first.

- To stay in the bedroom, go to page 79.
- To go to the kitchen for snacks, turn to page 82.

You and Tyler sit on one of the beds as you wait for Maggie to wash up. You notice a book next to the pillow. You open it and read a little about the inn.

"It says here that in the 1500s, they used to burn people at the stake," you tell Tyler.

"Like witches?" he asks.

"It says here that women were burned as suspected witches, and one of them hid here in the inn. She was captured and killed." You look at a photo in the book. It looks a lot like the room you're sitting in right now. Your eyes widen. "This room is called the witch's room! Tyler, she was caught here!"

As the words leave your mouth, the bathroom door swings open. Maggie stands at the doorway. Her face is as pale as the white towel she's holding.

Turn the page.

"I saw a woman in the mirror!" she says, pointing to the bathroom behind her.

The three of you huddle together on the bed. In the momentary silence, the room is filled with the sound of creaks and thumps.

"Maybe the house is settling for the night," you say, trying to comfort your friends and yourself.

Maggie shrieks, falling off the bed onto the floor.

You and Tyler help her up. As you look up again, a woman appears at the bathroom doorway. Her long dress is tattered, and her face is dirty with soot. She waves at you.

"That's the woman I saw!" Maggie squeals.

"It's the witch!" Tyler cries.

"We should get out of here," you say.

You reach the door first, but it's heavy and won't open. The three of you heave together, but it won't budge. You bang on the door with your fists, crying for help. The woman moves in closer. Her glare tells you she's not friendly.

"What are we going to do?" Tyler asks. You three have your backs pressed against the door as the ghost approaches.

An idea pops into your head. You could either beg for forgiveness or stand up to the ghost.

- To beg the ghost for mercy, turn to page 93.
- To stand up to the ghost, turn to page 96.

The bedroom is too quiet, and you lose your nerve. Following Tyler downstairs to get snacks sounds like a great idea. He leads you and Maggie down the heavy wooden staircase.

The kitchen is a large room with a low ceiling. Chairs and barrels used as tables fill the floor space. You glance at a stuffed ram's head. It gives you a creepy feeling. At the counter, there is an array of snacks.

"Do you think they set up scary events like in a haunted mansion at the fair?" Tyler asks, grabbing a handful of potato chips.

Before you can answer, you all hear a strange sound. It begins as a quiet sobbing, then grows into a tragic cry.

"It sounds like children," Maggie whispers.

Then something falls on the floor making a clanking sound. It glints in the dim lighting.

It's a dagger, a really old one.

"Where did that come from?" you cry.

"One of the articles I read about the inn mentioned that there were daggers discovered here many years ago, along with the bones of children," Maggie says, staring down at the knife. "People believed they were used in a ritual sacrifice of children."

Turn the page.

You bend down to get a closer look. "Do you think the owners placed it here as a trick to scare tourists?" You reach out to pick it up. Your fingers grip nothing.

"It's two-dimensional," you say, curious. "Clever."

Maggie and Tyler join you, running their hands over the dagger. "Cool trick," Maggie says.

The sound of crying grows louder. The lights flicker and go out. A wind gust blows through the room. But the windows are all shut tight.

Maggie screams. You scream. Tyler screams too. But part of you remembers this could all be a trick.

• To stay and investigate for signs of trickery, go to page 85.

• To run, turn to page 90.

"This is a really good trick," you say, swishing your hand over the dagger. "It's an optical illusion."

Maggie laughs nervously. She's not so convinced.

"I'll prove it," you say. You're convinced all this has to be trickery. No supernatural encounter can be this obvious. The videos you've watched about haunted houses show small temperature drops on devices, light drafts, or other minor signs of a possible ghost.

You use the flashlight on your phone to search for speakers and projectors. But you don't find anything.

"There must be something in here," you insist.

Turn the page.

But before you can say any more, you are thrown hard against the wall. Oof! Then Maggie and Tyler fly across the kitchen and hit a wall too. You all slide down onto the floor and sit dazed.

"What was that?" Tyler asks.

"My head hurts," Maggie says.

You've dropped your phone and crawl around in the darkness trying to find it. That's when you see her. A young woman rises from the kitchen floor and hovers over the three of you. Tear stains streak her dirty face as the sound of her moans fills the room.

"Don't hurt us," you plead. This is definitely not a trick.

You crawl over to your friends and grab their hands. Together, you run out of the kitchen into the reception area.

Sam is there, holding two bags of food. "I brought dinner," he says with a smile that quickly disappears as he sees the three of you. "What happened?" You explain to Sam what you saw.

"There have been reports of ghosts coming up through the floor," Sam says. "But I haven't heard of ghosts physically harming visitors in quite some time. I am so sorry that happened to you. Would you like to stay and eat? I promise I will be here to help you the rest of the night."

You look at your friends. They look hesitant. But your stomach is grumbling, and the food smells delicious.

- To stay and eat, turn to page 88.
- To prepare to leave, turn to page 99.

"I guess we may as well stay and eat," you say. "Thanks for dinner, Sam."

You, Tyler, and Maggie sit down at a table. The fish and chips are delicious. Everyone is pretty quiet, but you try to make polite conversation with your guide. Your friends are probably still thinking of the creepy ghost.

"I need to use the restroom," Maggie says, getting out of her seat.

When she comes back, her eyes are wide. "Um, do you have a visitor, Sam? I think I saw someone in the doorway over there." She points toward the reception area.

"No one else is here," Sam replies. "Let's go check it out."

You, Maggie, and Tyler nervously follow Sam out to the barn. You peer through the doorway.

Two blue orbs hover in the air in the middle of the barn. Suddenly, they fly toward you.

You turn and rush out the door. Maggie, Tyler, and Sam are right behind you.

You look at your friends. "That's it. I can't handle any more ghosts tonight." Your friends nod their heads. You say goodbye to Sam, relieved to leave the spooky inn far behind.

THE END

To follow another path, turn to page 9.
To learn more about haunted houses, turn to page 103.

Trick or no trick, you're too scared to find out. You run away. Your friends follow. You see a staircase and run up it. You pull open the first door you come to and dash inside. Tyler pulls the door shut.

You're in another bedroom. This one has red bedspreads and curtains too. Paintings hang on the walls.

"This is the bishop's room," Tyler says. "I read about it."

"Please don't tell me it's the most haunted room in the house," you say.

Before he can answer, you see a woman hanging from a rope by her legs. She's upside down!

You all scream.

A little dog appears in front of you. Its tongue hangs out as it pants.

"Do you see that?" you say, hoping it's your imagination.

"I hope it's friendly," Maggie says.

The dog hops onto a bed, which begins to lift off the floor.

Maggie screams again. You all dash down the stairs and out the front door. You run into the front garden and slam right into a body. Not another ghost!

It's Sam. "I brought dinner," he says, holding a shopping bag.

You tell him what happened between panicked breaths.

"I forgot to tell you that you have to knock three times before entering that room," he says. "Otherwise, you annoy the ghosts within."

Turn the page.

Sam tries to persuade you all to return to the inn with him. He promises not to leave you alone again.

You look at Maggie and Tyler. They're both pale with fear.

"Sorry, Sam," you say. "We've had enough."

Sam nods, with a sigh. "It's not easy encountering the spirits. Still, I hope you come back someday."

You wave politely, but don't reply. You're already heading toward Maggie's house. None of you talk about this experience for a long time.

THE END

To follow another path, turn to page 9.
To learn more about haunted houses, turn to page 103.

When you do something wrong at home, saying you're sorry seems to be the best way to get out of trouble. Surely, that could happen with angry ghosts, right?

You put both hands out in front of you. "We're sorry that we disturbed you! We really didn't mean to."

You squeeze your eyes shut and prepare to be attacked. But nothing happens. You open your eyes. The witch hasn't moved. She just watches you.

"What's happening?" Maggie whispers breathlessly.

The woman starts to cry. The cries grow into loud moaning sobs. The curtains flap, even though the windows are closed. The lights flicker.

Turn the page.

You're so nervous, words just spill out of you. "I think it's terrible that you had to die the way you did. But please don't be mad at us."

Suddenly, the room's lights grow brighter. There's no woman—just an ordinary bedroom. Begging for mercy has worked.

"See?" you say to your friends. You place your hand over your racing heart. "All she wanted was someone to understand her tragedy and to empathize."

Maggie hugs you. "I would never have had the presence of mind to do that. You did great."

You hear a knock on the bedroom door. When you open it, you see Sam. "Ready for adventure?" he asks. You tell him what happened.

"Looks like you found a way to appease the witch," he says, impressed. "The rest of this night will be a piece of cake for all of you then."

You shake your head. You've had enough. "I think we'll just head back to Maggie's house. This has been a wild experience."

Your friends agree. You spend the rest of the night talking it over in Maggie's safe, unhaunted bedroom.

THE END

To follow another path, turn to page 9.
To learn more about haunted houses, turn to page 103.

There's nowhere for you to go. You plant your feet and face the oncoming ghost.

"Stop!" you say as you put your hands out in front of you. "We will not be bullied by you."

Your heart pounds. The ghost flies at you with its mouth open wide.

Maggie shouts something, but you can't make out her words. Tyler grabs your shirt from behind and yanks you downward to the floor. You huddle in a tight pile, bracing yourselves.

The bedroom door swings open, and the three of you stumble out into the hallway.

You scramble to your feet. Tyler rushes to close the door before the ghost reaches you.

The door slams shut just as you hear a thud. Then you hear angry shrieks. The witch is letting you know she's furious. You're surprised she can't get through the door. Maybe she can't leave the room she haunts.

"That was close," Maggie says. "She was really angry."

Tyler whispers in disbelief. "What were you thinking?"

"I thought a show of strength might make her back down. I guess I was wrong." You rest your hands on your knees and try to catch your breath.

"Oh no!" you hear Sam say. He's stopped at the third step from the top of the staircase looking up at the three of you. "Did something happen?" You tell him about the ghost of the woman.

Turn the page.

Sam apologizes as you make your way down the stairs. "I would never have left you alone if I'd known this would happen. It's quite rare, I assure you."

You've decided this was enough of an encounter for the night—and for the rest of your lives.

"I'll have your bags delivered to your house tomorrow," Sam promises as you leave the inn.

You walk back to Maggie's house in silence. Her parents are surprised to see you, but they don't ask any questions. They must know you've encountered something awful.

THE END

To follow another path, turn to page 9.
To learn more about haunted houses, turn to page 103.

You look at your friends' faces. "I think we should pack up and leave. I'm sorry, Sam. I think we've all had enough spooky experiences for one night."

"I understand," Sam says. "Thinking about seeing ghosts is a lot different from actually encountering one."

As you pack, you glance at the stuffed animals on the bed. You freeze. Peeking out from between two stuffed animals are cat eyes. They belong to a black cat that is glaring back at you.

You scream. Your friends turn and see what you are staring at. The cat jumps at you. You raise your arms to cover your face. But nothing happens. When you look again, the cat is behind you on the floor. Its gleaming, sharp claws are exposed. It's crouched, ready to pounce again.

Turn the page.

You run out of the room and down the stairs. Your friends follow close behind.

Before you know it, you and your friends are in the front garden panting. You can't speak. It's too much.

Sam has followed you outside. "You saw something else?" he asks.

You can only nod. Your friends are already on their way down the sidewalk. You run after them and don't look back. There's no doubt the Ancient Ram Inn is haunted.

THE END

To follow another path, turn to page 9.
To learn more about haunted houses, turn to page 103.

CHAPTER 5
HAUNTED HOUSES

There are stories of haunted houses in almost every part of the world. People are drawn to haunted houses for many reasons. They may enjoy being frightened. Some are curious about the paranormal and what cannot be explained. Others are out to prove that hauntings aren't real. Many people think the stories can be explained by science and the natural world.

Ghost hunters look for signs of the paranormal as part of their work. They use instruments to assist in their investigations. These include EMF readers, special cameras, motion sensors, and thermometers. Ghost or spirit boxes scan radio frequencies to pick up the sounds of ghosts speaking.

Most encounters are not as obvious as the ones in this book. This often means that the experiences can be dismissed or explained away. Yet ghost hunters continue to seek out the unknown. Sometimes, events happen that just can't be explained.

Many stories about haunted houses have been told, and they span hundreds of years. People say they've seen the ghost of Annee Palmer riding a horse around the Rose Hall Great House property.

At the Winchester Mystery House, people have reported hearing voices. Chandeliers are said to sway for no reason.

At the Ancient Ram Inn, some people believe they have heard unseen children crying. People have reported seeing a ghost in the witch's room.

The spirits said to haunt these places lived in different countries and times. Yet many of them share the experience of tragedy in some way.

What do you think? Do you believe in ghosts? Or do you think science and other evidence can explain ghostly encounters? No matter what you think, there are many people who share your beliefs.

More Ghostly Encounters

There are many more haunted houses visitors can explore. The Whaley House in San Diego, California, is said to be haunted by the ghost of Jim Robinson. He was arrested in 1852 for many crimes, including horse theft and robbery. He was finally caught and killed as his punishment. Some people say his family and dog also haunt the house.

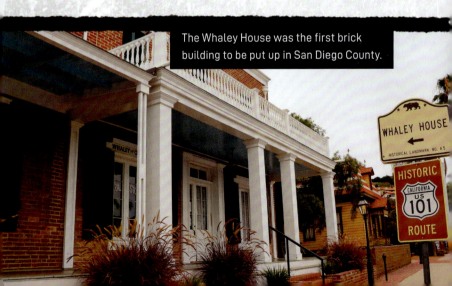

The Whaley House was the first brick building to be put up in San Diego County.

The White House where the U.S. president lives is also said to be haunted. People say they have seen the ghosts of past presidents who have lived there. Some say they have seen Abigail Adams, the wife of the second president, John Adams. They say she walks in the East Room carrying laundry. Some hear the voice of David Burns. He owned the land on which the White House was built. Presidents Andrew Jackson and Abraham Lincoln have also been seen wandering the halls of this great house.

The House of Death in New York City is a townhouse that is believed to be haunted by the ghosts of 22 people. One of them is a six-year-old girl who was murdered by her adoptive father. The famous writer Mark Twain is said to have lived there between 1900 and 1901. His spirit is also said to wander the halls.

Other Paths to Explore

What if you worked as a tour guide at a haunted house? Think about what you would need to know in order to provide a great experience to your tourists. If you saw a ghost while working there, would you keep working or would you quit?

Imagine you had the chance to buy an old, haunted house. Why would you want to own it? If you encountered a ghost there, would you try to communicate with it? Or would you run away?

Do some research and find the nearest haunted house in your town. What was the story behind it? Who might still be haunting the house?

Glossary

electromagnetic field (i-lik-troh-mag-NET-ik FEELD)—the space around a magnet or a planet like Earth, in which a magnetic force is active

infrared (in-fruh-RED)—a type of light that is invisible to human eyes

labyrinth (LA-buh-rinth)—a place full of passageways

medium (MEE-dee-uhm)—a person who claims to make contact with spirits of the dead

paranormal (pair-uh-NOR-muhl)—having to do with an unexplained event that has no scientific explanation

portal (POR-tuhl)—a doorway or entrance

renovation (ren-uh-VAY-shuhn)—the restoring of something to good condition

supernatural (soo-pur-NACH-ur-uhl)—something that cannot be given an ordinary explanation

Victorian (vik-TOR-ee-uhn)—relating to large, decorative houses built during the reign of Queen Victoria in England

voodoo (VOO-doo)—a religion that began in Africa

Select Bibliography

Bagans, Zak, and Kelly Crigger. *Dark World: Into the Shadows with the Lead Investigator of the Ghost Adventures Crew.* Las Vegas, NV: Victory Belt Publishing, 2011.

Botz, Corinne May. *Haunted Houses.* New York: The Monacelli Press, 2010.

Inside the World's Most Haunted Houses. Mazz Appeal Films, 2020.

Lecouteux, Claude. *The Tradition of Household Spirits: Ancestral Lore and Practices.* Rochester, VT: Inner Traditions, 2013.

Naylor, Celia E. *Unsilencing Slavery: Telling Truths about Rose Hall Plantation, Jamaica.* Athens, GA: University of Georgia Press, 2022.

Rose Hall Great House
rosehall.com

Winchester Mystery House
winchestermysteryhouse.com

Read More

Carlson-Berne, Emma. *Haunted History.* Minneapolis: Lerner Publishing, 2024.

Chandler, Matt. *Ghosts of the O.K. Corral and Other Hauntings of Tombstone, Arizona.* North Mankato, MN: Capstone, 2021.

Hoena, Blake. *The Deadly Bell Witch Ghost: A Ghostly Graphic.* North Mankato, MN: Capstone, 2024.

Internet Sites

The Amazing Story Behind England's Haunted Ancient Ram Inn and Reasons to Visit
travelawaits.com/2480927/england-haunted-ancient-ram-inn

Rose Hall Great House
rosehall.com

Top 10 Most Haunted Houses in the World
theworldbucketlist.com/top-ten-most-haunted-houses-in-the-world

About the Author

Ailynn Collins has written many books for children, from stories about aliens and monsters, to books about science, space, and the future. These are her favorite subjects. She lives outside Seattle with her family and five dogs. When she's not writing, she enjoys participating in dog shows and dog sports.